Winged Return to Paradise. The author arriving in Hawaii by Clipper from California.

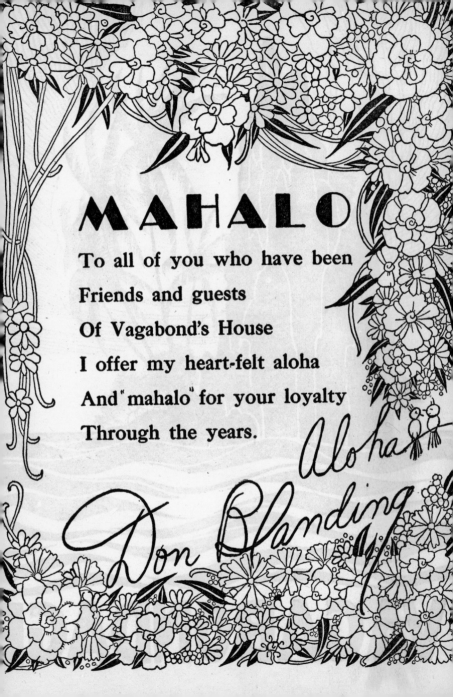

MAHALO

To all of you who have been

Friends and guests

Of Vagabond's House

I offer my heart-felt aloha

And "mahalo" for your loyalty

Through the years.

Aloha

Don Blanding

VAGABONDAGE

Acknowledgment is made to the Honolulu Star Bulletin, the Honolulu Advertiser, M. Kawahara, Henry Inn, Ching Chong the Candlemaker and Patten Co. Ltd., for the use of some of my verses.

To the restless ones . . .
To all the gallant frantic fools
Who follow the path of the sun
Across blue waters
To distant mountains
I dedicate my book.

VAGABOND'S HOUSE

By

DON BLANDING

Illustrations by the Author

New York

DODD, MEAD & COMPANY

1946

PRINTED IN THE UNITED STATES OF AMERICA
BY THE VAIL-BALLOU PRESS, INC., BINGHAMTON, N. Y.

VAGABOND'S HOUSE
GUEST BOOK

THE BOOKS OF
DON BLANDING
ILLUSTRATIONS BY THE AUTHOR

PREFACE

Vagabond's Road

Not for all the lonely winding road that leads across the
    hill
Into the neverness beyond. And not for all the restless
    thrill
Of changing skies. Only for him who knows the cease-
    less urge
To go . . . go ever on, carried by tide and trade-wind's
    pulsing surge,
Lured by the bright mirage of far-off places,
Forests and jungles and bleak frozen spaces,
Ready to bid love greeting or farewell
With the same light gesture. Knowing the spell
That makes the Somewhere-else the Promised Land,
Caring no whit if Sun of Surr or Samarkand
Shall bleach his bones or curious creatures of the sea
Play havoc with his flesh. Content to be
Lover of Chance with Loneliness for wife,
Faithful to faithlessness of all save life,
Ready to face that last dim misted trail
When eager eyes and pliant muscles fail,
Thinking of Death as just another place to go,
Another road to walk, another land to know.

CONTENTS

12

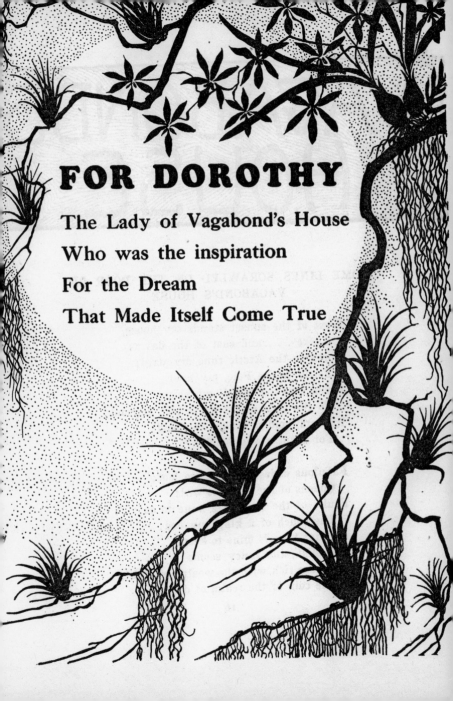

FOR DOROTHY

The Lady of Vagabond's House
Who was the inspiration
For the Dream
That Made Itself Come True

VAGABOND'S HOUSE

SOME LINES SCRAWLED ON THE DOOR OF VAGABOND'S HOUSE

West of the sunset stands my house,
    There . . . and east of the dawn;
North to the Arctic runs my yard;
    South to the Pole, my lawn;
Seven seas are to sail my ships
    To the ends of the earth . . . beyond;
Drifters' gold is for me to spend
    For I am a vagabond.

Fabulous cities are mine to loot;
    Queens of the earth to wed;
Fruits of the world are mine to eat;
    The couch of a king, my bed;
All that I see is mine to keep;
    Foolish, the fancy seems
But I am rich with the wealth of Sight,
    The coin of the realm of dreams.

VAGABOND'S HOUSE

When I have a house . . . as I sometime may . . .
I'll suit my fancy in every way.
I'll fill it with things that have caught my eye
In drifting from Iceland to Molokai.
It won't be correct or in period style
But . . . oh, I've thought for a long, long while
Of all the corners and all the nooks,
Of all the bookshelves and all the books,
The great big table, the deep soft chairs
And the Chinese rug at the foot of the stairs,
(it's an old, old rug from far Chow Wan
that a Chinese princess once walked on).

My house will stand on the side of a hill
By a slow broad river, deep and still,
With a tall lone pine on guard nearby
Where the birds can sing and the storm winds cry.
A flagstone walk with lazy curves
Will lead to the door where a Pan's head serves
As a knocker there like a vibrant drum
To let me know that a friend has come,
And the door will squeak as I swing it wide
To welcome you to the cheer inside.

For I'll have good friends who can sit and chat
Or simply sit, when it comes to that,
By the fireplace where the fir logs blaze
And the smoke rolls up in a weaving haze.

I'll want a wood-box, scarred and rough,
For leaves and bark and odorous stuff
Like resinous knots and cones and gums
To chuck on the flames when winter comes.
And I hope a cricket will stay around
For I love its creaky lonesome sound.

There'll be driftwood powder to burn on logs
And a shaggy rug for a couple of dogs,
Boreas, winner of prize and cup,
And Micky, a loveable gutter-pup.
Thoroughbreds, both of them, right from the start,
One by breeding, the other by heart.

.　　.　　.　　.　　.　　.　　.

There are times when only a dog will do
For a friend . . . when you're beaten, sick and blue
And the world's all wrong, for he won't care
If you break and cry, or grouch and swear,
For he'll let you know as he licks your hands
That he's downright sorry . . . and understands.

I'll have on a bench a box inlaid
With dragon-plaques of milk-white jade
To hold my own particular brand
Of cigarettes brought from the Pharaoh's land
With a cloisonne bowl on a lizard's skin
To flick my cigarette ashes in.
And a squat blue jar for a certain blend
Of pipe tobacco. I'll have to send
To a quaint old chap I chanced to meet
In his fusty shop on a London street.

   A long low shelf of teak will hold
My best-loved books in leather and gold
While magazines lie on a bowlegged stand
In a polyglot mixture close at hand.
   I'll have on a table a rich brocade
That I think the pyxies must have made
For the dull gold thread on blues and grays
Weaves the pattern of Puck . . . the Magic Maze.
   On the mantelpiece I'll have a place
For a little mud god with a painted face
That was given to me . . . oh, long ago
By a Philippine maid in Olongapo.

Then . . . just in range of a lazy reach . . .
A bulging bowl of Indian beech
Will brim with things that are good to munch,
Hickory nuts to crack and crunch,
Big fat raisins and sun-dried dates
And curious fruits from the Malay Straits,
Maple sugar and cookies brown
With good hard cider to wash them down,
Wine-sap apples, pick of the crop,
And ears of corn to shell and pop
With plenty of butter and lots of salt . . .
If you don't get filled it's not my fault.

   And there where the shadows fall I've planned
To have a magnificent Concert-Grand
With polished wood and ivory keys
For wild discordant rhapsodies,
For wailing minor Hindu songs,
For Chinese chants with clanging gongs,
For flippant jazz and for lullabies
And moody things that I'll improvise
To play the long gray dusk away
And bid good-bye to another day.

Pictures . . . I think I'll have but three;
One, in oil, of a wind-swept sea
With the flying scud and the waves whipped white . . .
(I know the chap who can paint it right)
In lapis blue and a deep jade green . . .
A great big smashing fine marine
That'll make you feel the spray in your face.
I'll hang it over my fireplace.

The second picture . . . a freakish thing . . .
Is gaudy and bright as a macaw's wing,
An impressionistic smear called "Sin,"
A nude on a striped zebra skin
By a Danish girl I knew in France.
My respectable friends will look askance
At the purple eyes and the scarlet hair,
At the pallid face and the evil stare
Of the sinister beautiful vampire face.
I shouldn't have it about the place
But I like . . . while I loathe . . . the beastly thing
And that's the way that one feels about sin.

The picture I love the best of all
Will hang alone on my study wall
Where the sunset's glow and the moon's cold gleam
Will fall on the face and make it seem
That the eyes in the picture are meeting mine,
That the lips are curved in the fine sweet line
Of that wistful, tender, provocative smile
That has stirred my heart for a wondrous while.

It's a sketch of the girl who loved too well
To tie me down to that bit of Hell
That a drifter knows when he finds he's held
By the soft strong chains that passions weld.

It was best for her and for me, I know,
That she measured my love and bade me go
For we both have our great illusion yet
Unsoiled, unspoiled by a vain regret.
I won't deny that it makes me sad
To know that I've missed what I might have had.
It's a clean sweet memory, quite apart,
And I've been faithful . . . in my heart.

All these things I will have about,
Not a one could I do without;
Cedar and sandalwood chips to burn
In the tarnished bowl of a copper urn,
A paperweight of meteorite
That seared and scorched the sky one night,
A Moro kris . . . my paperknife . . .
Once slit the throat of a Rajah's wife.

The beams of my house will be fragrant wood
That once in a teeming jungle stood
As a proud tall tree where the leopards couched
And the parrot screamed and the black men crouched.
The roof must have a rakish dip
To shadowy eaves where the rain can drip
In a damp, persistent tuneful way;
It's a cheerful sound on a gloomy day.
And I want a shingle loose somewhere
To wail like a banshee in despair
When the wind is high and the storm-gods race
And I am snug by my fireplace.

I hope a couple of birds will nest
Around the house. I'll do my best
To make them happy, so every year
They'll raise their brood of fledglings here.

When I have my house I will suit myself
And have what I'll call my "Condiment Shelf"
Filled with all manner of herbs and spice,
Curry and chutney for meats and rice,
Pots and bottles of extracts rare . . .
Onions and garlic will both be there. . . .
And soyo and saffron and savory-goo
And stuff that I'll buy from an old Hindu,
Ginger with syrup in quaint stone jars,
Almonds and figs in tinselled bars,
Astrakhan caviar, highly prized,
And citron and orange peel crystallized,
Anchovy paste and poha jam,
Basil and chili and marjoram,
Pickles and cheeses from every land
And flavors that come from Samarkand.

And, hung with a string from a handy hook,
Will be a dog-eared, well-thumbed book
That is pasted full of recipes
From France and Spain and the Caribbees,
Roots and leaves and herbs to use
For curious soups and odd ragouts.

I'll have a cook that I'll name Oh Joy,
A sleek, fat, yellow-faced China boy
Who can roast a pig or mix a drink,
(you can't improve on a slant-eyed Chink).

24

On the gray-stone hearth there'll be a mat
For a scrappy, swaggering yellow cat
With a war-scarred face from a hundred fight
With neighbors' cats on moonlight nights.
A wise old Tom who can hold his own
And make my dogs let him alone.

I'll have a window-seat broad and deep
Where I can sprawl to read or sleep,
With windows placed so I can turn
And watch the sunsets blaze and burn
Beyond high peaks that scar the sky
Like bare white wolf-fangs that defy
The very gods. I'll have a nook
For a savage idol that I took
From a ruined temple in Peru,
A demon-chaser named Mang-Chu
To guard my house by night and day
And keep all evil things away.

Pewter and bronze and hammered brass,
Old carved wood and gleaming glass,
Candles in polychrome candlesticks
And peasant lamps in floating wicks,
Dragons in silk on a Mandarin suit
In a chest that is filled with vagabond-loot.
All of the beautiful useless things
That a vagabond's aimless drifting brings.

. . . Then when my house is all complete
I'll stretch me out on the window seat
With a favorite book and a cigarette
And a long cool drink that Oh Joy will get
And I'll look about at my bachelor-nest
While the sun goes zooming down the west
And the hot gold light will fall on my face
And make me think of some heathen place
That I've failed to see . . . that I've missed some
    way . . .
A place that I'd planned to find some day,
And I'll feel the lure of it drawing me.
Oh damn! I know what the end will be.
I'll go. And my house will fall away
While the mice by night and the moths by day
Will nibble the covers off all my books
And the spiders weave in the shadowed nooks
And my dogs . . . I'll see that they have a home
While I follow the sun, while I drift and roam
To the ends of the earth like a chip on the stream,
Like a straw on the wind, like a vagrant dream,
And the thought will strike with a swift sharp pain
That I probably never will build again
This house that I'll have in some far day.
Well . . . it's just a dream-house anyway.

GOLD

My treasure chest is filled with gold.
       Gold . . . gold . . . gold.
Vagabond's gold and drifter's gold . . .
Worthless, priceless dreamer's gold . . .
Gold of the sunset . . . gold of the dawn . . .
Gold of the shower trees on my lawn . . .
Poet's gold and artist's gold . . .
Gold that can not be bought or sold. . . .
       Gold.

NAMES ARE SHIPS

Names! The lure in names of places
Stirring thoughts of foreign faces,
Ports and palaces and steamers.
Names are ships to carry dreamers.

  Pago-pago, Suva, Java,
  Languor, lotuses and lava,
Everything a dreamer wishes,
Buried treasure, flying fishes,
Cocoanuts and kings and corals,
Pirates, pearls and pagan morals,
Rum and reefs and Christian teaching,
Gin, and jungle parrots screeching.

  Kobe, Nikko, Yokohama,
  Views of sacred Fujiyama,
Bales of silk and bowls of lacquer,
Dragons on a sugar cracker,
Temples high on pictured mountains,
Purple gold-fish, perfume fountains,
Amber, obis, geisha dances,
Almond eyes and slanted glances.

28

Places that I pray I may go,
    Rio, Terra del Fuego,
Condors soaring in the Andes,
Cloying Guatemalan candies,
Pampas grasses, pink flamingos,
Spanish girls who call us "gringos,"
Llamas, lizards, smoking craters,
Armadillos, alligators.

    Cairo, Carthage, Congo . . . CONGO!
    Names that like a savage gong go,
Paris, Venice, gay Vienna,
Cocottes' kisses, genius, henna,
Gorgeous vicious mad Manhattan,
Misery, motors, rags and satin,
Moose and mice and sin and sago,
Yaps from Yap or Winnebago.

    Every name a ship with cargo,
    Brass from Burmah, wheat from Fargo,
Pots and prunes and precious metal
Mined on Popocatapetl,
Chests of carved and stained catalpa,
Letters from Tegucigalpa,
Linen from an Irish shanty
For a store in Ypsilanti

Sailing ship and ocean liner
Bringing stuff from Asia Minor,
Ferry boat or lazy freighter,
Folks from China or Decatur,
Mozambique or Madagascar,
Slav or Serb or savage Lascar,
Barber, Berber or Brazilian
Clad in blue or bright vermilion.

Fascinating names of places
Stirring thoughts of foreign faces,
Ports and palaces and steamers,
Names are ships to carry dreamers.

P. S. There's a place I want to go,
A place called Paramaribo.
I don't know and I don't care
Where it is or who lives there
But just as sure as Fate I know
I'll go to Paramaribo.

DRIFTWOOD

Never a tide goes out to sea
But carries a bit of the heart of me
Riding the foam and the gray sea-wrack,
Caring no whit if it ne'er comes back,
Drifting over the seven seas
Driven by trade-wind, storm and breeze,
Hearing the cry of the sad sea-loon,
Floating a while in a blue lagoon,
Bleached and scorched by the tropic suns,
Spun away when the rip-tide runs,
On and over and back and forth
Up to the still white frozen north
Where a weary day is a long half year
And out of the icebergs dead men peer.
Hither and thither and on and yon,
Glamorous night and clamorous dawn,
Gaining nothing and losing less,
Loving the joy, accepting the stress,
Taking whatever the Fates may give.
God, it's a glorious life to live.

WILD GEESE

I remember . . . how could I forget . . .
  The first faint beating of rebellious wings
Within my heart. Youngster, I had not yet
  Gone forth on high adventurings
      Beyond the pages of a book. One day
        A bronze and amber autumn afternoon
      Teasing my mind with idle dreams I lay
        Watching the sun die red, waiting the moon.

Suddenly a hoarse and vibrant cry
  Riddled the air with strong staccato might
And there across the sultry burning sky
  Soared the great cleaving "V" of geese in flight,
      Racing the winter winds. And like a spell
        Their wing-song challenged me. My eager heart
      Rose in response to follow . . . fluttered . . .
        fell . . .
        Baffled, reluctant after that brave start.

I made a thousand small increasing trials
  Each stronger, surer, longer than the last
Until gay spring with myriad flower-smiles
  Routed the gods of snow . . . and winter passed.
      Then when the first awaited warning call
        Drummed down the sky I spread young lusty
          wings
        Triumphantly in flight beyond recall
          Of faithfulness to aught save far horizons'
            beckonings.

CENTAUR

I wonder if, long centuries ago,
I was a centaur for somehow I know
That once I led my wild stampeding herd
Of milk-white mares and colts. Our hoofbeats stirred
The bronzy Grecian hillsides into dust.
My neighing challenge, strong with living lust,
Rang out, a cry half human and half brute,
Across lush meadows. From a nearby butte
A nightblack stallion answered with discordant scream
And raged to battle.   This I did not dream
For I can feel the thundered shock as bodies met,
Foam flecked. I sense the rancid reek of sweat,
I see flared nostrils, red distended eyes
And hear the blended dissonance of furious cries.

  I, with brute passion joined with human skill,
Reared, lunged and struck . . . struck true to kill.
With slashing hoof I ripped the swollen vein
That laced my rival's throat. A gasp of pain,
A strong convulsive shudder, and a pulsing flood
Gushed forth to bathe me in thick crimson blood.
Then whinnying triumph, with pride-lifted head,
Back to my white submissive mares I sped.

SONG OF THE SENSES

This is the five-stringed harp, the singing lyre,
  To play the mad sweet song I improvise,
  My life, song of the senses; to devise
New harmonies and chords. I never tire
    Questioning the taunt responsive strings
     For overtones of sensuous delight,
      Blending the five, taste, touch, scent, hearing,
        sight,
      Hushing my breath to catch the faintest whisper-
        ings.

To feel . . . the subtleties of silk, the suave caress
  Of satin, warmth of amber, chill of jade,
  The sinister temptation of a dagger blade,
The sluggishness of lead, a body's suppleness,
    The luxury of fur, the gauzy mesh
     Of spiderwebs, the yielding of curved lips;
     If I were blind my straying fingertips
    Would know the velvet texture of white flesh.

To hear . . . dull muffled thunder in the sky,
  The thin sweet note that bells of Chinese jade
  Give off when struck with silver. Cannonade
Of surf on coral reefs, a gull's lone cry,
    Gongs, cymbals, zithers that wild gypsies strum,
     A muted laugh, a shrilled harsh shriek of fear;
     If I were deaf I know my heart would hear
    The challenge of a far-off beaten drum.

To see . . . ah, God, to see new skies, new lands,
  Strange cities, temples, palaces, blue seas,
  Old flags, defiant, whipping in the breeze,
Red flowers, forests standing, desert sands,
    Bazaars ablaze with color, pageantry,
      White peacocks, people, porphyry and brass,
      Clouds, crystal, ivory, ebony and glass;
    Fate, grant me this, that I may always see!

To breathe the musk of life, the strong perfume
  Of living things, trees, flowers, ripened fruit,
  The honest smell of onions, orrisroot,
The friendly scent of old familiar rooms,
    Leaves burning of an autumn afternoon,
      Mint, myrrh, magnolia, cinnamon and cloves,
      White jasmine, juniper and orange groves,
    The thousand summer fragrances of June.

To taste . . . good food, meats, sauces, gravies, spice,
  Hot chilis, syrups, honey and fresh bread,
  Crisp ham, wild game, thick steaks, rare, juicy, red,
Odd relishes that epicures devise;
    To drink light beer and dark from wooden kegs,
      White wine and red, . . . champagne if I prefer,
      Fresh milk, cold water or an old liqueur,
    But wine of wines to drink . . . Life, froth and
      dregs.

35

THE POET AND THE WOMAN

A Study in Memories

The poet speaks.
　That night beneath a waning moon a pallid pool
　Slumbered in lotus-burdened beauty, crystal cool.
　　　　　　　　　　Do you remember . . .

The woman answers.
　I remember that at first your lips were cool
　But warmed to the ardent flame of mine, there by the
　　　pool.

The poet speaks.
　Clusters of stars were mirrored there like jewels of
　　　light
　And pale moonflowers mocked the moon with per-
　　　fumed white.
　　　　　　　　　　Do you remember . . .

The woman answers.
　I remember two hot stars blazed in your eyes.
　The fragrance of your flesh was sweeter than a
　　　flower could devise.

The poet speaks.
　All through the swooning night a lonely night-in-gale
　Sang the mad rapture of its heartbreak 'til the moon
　　　grew pale.
　　　　　　　　　　Do you remember . . .

The woman answers.
　I remember that the silent singing of my heart
　Held thrice more poignant sorrow than a bird's song
　　　could impart.

The poet speaks.
  Dawn was a radiance, smoky mauve and drifting gold,
  Crying with beauty that the pagan gods alone behold.
                              Do you remember . . .
The woman answers.
  I remember that the dawn was gray with pain
  Ending a night I knew could never come to me again.

DRIFTER

I am bloodbrother of all drifting things
That ride the wind and tide, or on swift wings
Cry down the pathless blackness of the nights,
Guided by restlessness and phantom lights
Of will-o'-the-wisps borne by lost frantic souls,
Futile seekers of far shifting goals.
  We see strange sights, learn curious truths,
Find lotus lands and taste the fruit that soothes
Our fretted spirits for a blissful while
In vague enchantment on an idle dreaming isle,
But leaves us craving, seeking once again
Veiled distances. We know the stabbing pain
That makes the desolation-haunting loon
Fling maniac laughter to the silent moon,
For once, god-cursed, it saw the monstrous joke
Life plays on life; its terrored reason broke
And so its mocking mirth congeals our blood.
We are the riders of the aimless flood,

Strayed human driftwood watching with wise weary
    eyes
The brassy tropic suns and shallow empty skies
Of chartless seas. One day is like another day,
And we unhappy, happy . . . who can say?
We know not what strange port shall be our last,
Nor care. Today we feast, tomorrow fast.
The treasure found is less to us than treasure sought,
And we most dearly treasure trifles dearly bought,
While all those tender things, love, friendship, home
That haunt the dreams of us who drift and roam
We trade for worthless star-dust which we vainly seek
In nameless valleys lost behind some mist-enshrouded
    peak.

Just this side of Somewhere there's a lovely lonely
island,
  A lotus-languid island in a molten opal sea,
The mountains there are jasper, jade and jasper are the
mountains;
    There's a pearl and purple palace that I've built for
    you and me.

On a beach of gold and topaz there's a pearly purple
palace;
  The halls are paved with onyx and the walls are
  figured brass;
There are cages filled with leopards, sullen leopards,
black and tawny;
    There are parakeets and macaws perched on trees of
    gilt and glass.

There are canopies of moonstones, hollow moonstones
filled with seed-pearls
  Where the breeze can sigh and tinkle and the moonlight filter through
To the couch where you are sleeping on a coverlet of
silver
  While a night-in-gale is singing muted lullabies to
  you.

In the dawn I'll come and wake you, with a song of
love I'll wake you,
  Then we'll stroll down stairs of porphyry inlaid with
  malachite,
While the white fantastic peacocks spread their gauzy
fans to shield us

From the fervor and the brightness of the dawn's
    hot gilding light.
In a shallow pool of turquoise where the pallid lilies
    slumber
  We will drift and dream in languor as the hours flow
    away,
Watching dragon-flies and orchids, counting idle glid-
    ing bubbles,
  Doing nothing most delightfully throughout the sum-
    mer day.

I have made a boat of wishes and it's ready for our
    sailing,
  The oars are teak and sandalwood, the sails are woven
    gold,
Across a sea of moonlight with the evening star to
    guide us
  We will float until the distant jasper mountains we
    behold.

A RESPONSE

I wrote of my house of dreams one day,
My "Vagabond's House." I told the way
That the rugs were laid across the floor,
I told of the walls and the panelled door,
I told of the books on a teak-wood stand,
The bits of lacquer, the Concert-Grand,
The favorite pictures on the wall,
The woven silk of a faded shawl,
The jars of spices along a shelf,
I told of the things I chose myself
To grace my house . . . those priceless things
That an hour of idle dreaming brings.
  So vividly real it sometimes seemed
That I quite forgot that I only dreamed;
That the walls were smoke, that the colors gay
Were a dear mirage that would fade away.

So I wrote as though the house were real.
The book went forth and made appeal
To some far person in some far land.
I know, for a letter came to hand. . . .

"Dear Friend," it said, "I don't know you,
But I am a dreamer and vagabond, too,
And the house you built of fragile stuff
Is the same as mine. If we dream enough,
If we strive and work, I truly feel
That we can make our houses *real*.
And if mine comes true and I build some day
A house of wood or stone or clay
In a summer land by a drowsy sea
I hope you will come and visit me
For the door will open to rooms beyond
For poet and artist and vagabond,
A cozy chair and the table set,
A book and a drink and a cigarette,
A shaded light with an orange glow . . .
All of the things we love and know.
  It may be never, it may be soon
But I hope that maybe some afternoon
I'll hear a step on the creaking stair . . .
I'll open the door and you'll be there.
                    Yours, a vagabond.

Address . . .
      "A God-forgotten Spot," South Africa.

44

DREAMER

I don't suppose I'll ever see
A dryad slipping from her tree
Nor hear the pulsing pipes of Pan
(although at times I think I can)
Nor see the moon-nymphs dance at night
And yet, perhaps . . . perhaps I might.

I watch the waves break on the rocks
And, in between the thundered shocks
I think that I can almost hear
The sirens singing sweet and clear.

Sometimes the shadows on a tree
Like dappled fauns appear to me
And once beside a blue lagoon
Beneath a witching tropic moon
I saw the flash of silver scales
(the kind that grow on mermaids' tails)

I don't suppose I'll ever see
These things that mean so much to me
But if I watch by night, by day,
You can not tell . . . perhaps I may.

JADE

AND

JOSS

THE CANDLEMAKER

A cubby-hole, dark dingy gray
   Tucked in between two little stores
    With stagnant tubs of fish about
    And bowls of Chinese sauerkraut
   And vegetables strewn on the floors
The candle-maker sits all day.

He looks as old as time itself,
   His face is but a wrinkled mask,
    Thin body, like a gargoyle bent
    Above his pools of paint, content.
   To dream in paint and wax, his task.
The dreams, as candles, line a shelf

With tallow fat on bamboo wicks,
    With patterns from a 'broidered shawl,
        With careful brush and Chinese skill
        He works his wizardry until
    Strange flowers bloom and dragons crawl
Along fantastic candlesticks.

A sudden thick vermilion splash,
    A subtle green that has no name,
        A wavered line of antique gold,
        Cerise, celestial blue . . . behold!
    A phœnix rises from the flame
Where seven colors shriek and clash.

"Good luck, long life" is written there
    Upon each stick in letters bold.
        So in your painted candle's glow
        Wherever you may be, you'll know
    The curling blue-gray smoke will hold
For you a kindly Chinese prayer.

And with the smoke your thoughts will stray
    To where, between two little stores
        With stagnant tubs of fish about
        And bowls of Chinese sauerkraut
    And vegetables strewn on the floors
The candle-maker paints all day.

CHINESE MUSIC

Eee-e-e—yih—Bong! and a
  clat-a-clat-a-clat and a Bong!
    I can hear them scraping on a cat-gut nerve. . . .
    I can hear them beating on a gong. . . .
    Like the brazen curse
    Of a bilious god. . . .
      BONG!

clat-a-clat-a-clat and a clat-a-clat-a-clat
  Like a goat-hoofed devil on the roof of my mind
  I can hear them beating with a stick. . . .
    Like a dry, hard pulse
    In a wooden vein
      clat-a-clat-a-clat

eee-yih—a-ah and an eee-yih—a-ah and a
      BONG!
  Like a screech of a tooth with an ache and a voice
  In a shrill falsetto like a pain . . .
    Like the scratch of a pin
    On a blistered wrist
      eee-ee-yih-a-ah!

JEWEL-TREES

Now I know where the jewel-trees grow,
Where blossoms of rose-carnelian blow
On twisted branches of weathered gold
And pale pink petals of quartz unfold
To show white stamens tipped with pearls
While lapis-lazuli leaves in swirls
With slivers of paper-thin jade surround
Fat amber buds. The glittering ground
Is flaked with coral-petal flower snow.
In cloisonné bowls the jewel-trees grow.
In a window of Fong Inn's store they bear
Their burden of beauty. Go see them there.

Musty, fusty, dusty smells
Gilded gods and temple bells,
Candlesticks of twisted brass,
Teak and ebony and glass.

Silks
Slinky, slithery silks . . .
That hiss and shimmer as Ah Moy stirs them;
Light from a painted lantern blurs them.
Soft whispering silks. . . .
Heavy murmurous silks . . .
Celestial blues
Rainbow hues
Many silks.
And little boxes.
Red lacquered pigskin.
Brass boxes from Thibet, studded with turquoise.
Raw turquoise and white jade.
Boxes that a blind man made,
Feeling with scarred sensitive fingers
For the design
And twisting line
Of the dragon's tail.

Fragile ivory boxes, delicate as lace, holding kingfisher
    feathers, jewelry and necklaces and earrings and
    tiny flowers made of silver shavings and gold wire
    and seed-pearls.

Red, red lacquer
And black lacquer flecked with gold
And traced with the name of the Emperor.
Glass beads,
Carved seeds,
Chains of Peking Liu
Twilight blue. . . .
Amber beads like globes of honeyed sunlight, warm to
    the touch, strung on orange silk.
White light flicked from points of silver filagree.

Many eyes.
Eyes of little porcelain dogs
Brightly inquisitive.
Eyes of dragons in silk on a Mandarin suit.
Flaming eyes. . . .
Slanted unwinking eyes of Chow Fat
Like black beads with lights behind them.

Chow Fat, the proprietor,
His face is like old leather
And his smile is kindly
And wise.
His fingers are very long . . . and pointed.

Behind Chow Fat are the eyes of Buddha,
The calm gilded eyes of Buddha.
Their tranquillity soothes unrest.

. . . .

Musty, fusty, dusty smells,
Gilded gods and temple bells
And the dull monotonous song
Of a brass gong.

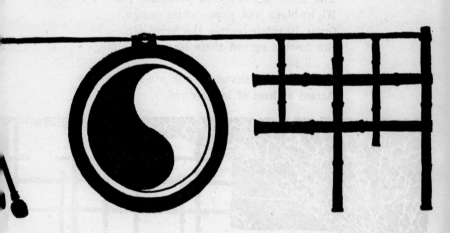

CHINESE SHAWLS

Three Chinese shawls of silk are spread
Across a chest of lacquer red.

One shawl is black, with poison green
And jade and blue ultramarine . . .
Fantastic flowers, shrill cerise
In exquisite embroideries.

Another shawl is oyster white.
Exotic blossoms there invite
Strange butterflies to 'light and fold
Their wings of powdered Chinese gold.

The third is strange in patterned line . . .
Night-black and paper-white design,
Quite Beardsleyesque, the very same
Sin-flowers spread their leaves of flame.

These Chinese shawls of silk are spread
Across a chest of lacquer red.

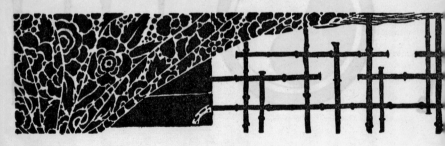

CORAL

AND

LAVA

LEAVES FROM MY GRASS-HOUSE

My grass-house stands by the open sea
On a bit of beach that belongs to me,
And I paid . . . I don't remember the price
Of my little acre in Paradise.

Now, a great deal more than sun-browned leaves
Of Island grass went into the weaves
And walls of my house, for all day long
As we built the house there were scraps of song
And tatters of laughter and wisps of sighs
All tangled up with the binding ties
Of love and friendliness. Wondrous things
Were used to make my house. The strings
Of my heart were the warp, my love the woof
Of woven walls and brown-thatched roof

Oh, the Southern Cross hangs over my door
And the moon flings silver on the floor
While the surf makes thunder along the beach
And the rainbow's end is within my reach.

The jasmine sprinkles my walls with stars
And spend-thrift sun-gold lies in bars
On the *hala* mat where I sprawl at ease
And feel the swift caressing breeze
That is tanged with salt from the lazy sea
Where the flying fish skim endlessly.

By looking beyond my window ledge
I can see a long hibiscus hedge
With polka-dot pattern of red and white
Aquiver with life in the drenching light.

The green fantastic mountains rise
In sudden swoops to the startled skies
Where white cloud-monsters puff their cheeks
And scrape their bellies across the peaks.

Along the reef on a still dark night
A fisherman prowls with a flaring light
Of smoky orange. He peers and feels
In the coral caves for the tiger-eels
And the slimy squid. He brings to me
Crisp wet *limu* cooled by the sea,
And little sea-urchins full of meat
And lobsters and crabs for me to eat.

There's a monkey-pod tree upon my lawn
Where the mynah birds, at the peep of dawn
Raise an awful row, but I don't care.
I rather like to hear them there.

Oh, the seasons come and the seasons go,
And the kona-storms and the trade-winds blow.
While the mangoes ripen on the trees
And I smell white ginger in the breeze.
The breadfruit swings its swollen globes
Of luscious green. Like royal robes
The gorgeous bougainvillea spreads
Its scarlet and magenta reds.

All up and down the road in rows
The autumn-colored croton grows
In red and green and russet-brown.
A little stream comes rushing down
Across my yard. I dammed it so
The water hyacinths could grow.

In June the reckless shower trees
Spend all their hoarded wealth to please
My fancy with a dress of gold
While poinciana, wanton-bold

Bedecks itself with flaming red.
The pale begonia flowers shed
A pearly pinkish sort of dew
Of petals on the grass. Can you
Look through my eyes and see this land
Where beauty lives on every hand?
And would you care to use my ears
And hear the music with its tears
Beneath a joyous note? I'll give
My heart to you so you may live
One day in Paradise. My hut
Of grass is open to you, but
I think before the day has flown
You'll want a grass house of your own.

Oh, little grass house on the beach
Your drifting wind-blown leaves will reach
Across the world, across the years
And settle on my heart. The fears
Of losing you have made me care
To pluck a leaf from here and there
And weave them into lazy line
And keep them in this book of mine.

POI

A very gooey paste which takes the place of bread at Hawaiian *luaus* or feasts and is eaten with the fingers. It is called "one-finger, two-finger or three-finger" poi according to its consistency.

One-finger, two-finger, three-finger poi!
Go to a *luau* and eat it with joy.
Eat it with *laulau* and eat it with *limu;*
Eat it with hunks of roast pig from the *imu;*
Eat it with breadfruit and big sweet potatoes;
Eat it with salmon fixed up with tomatoes;
Eat it with chicken . . . it's better with mullet
Which tickles your palate and pleases your gullet;
    Don't use a fork . . .
    Wiggle your finger
    Deep in the poi-bowl . . .
    Lift it, don't linger.
Give it a flip in the proper direction,
It gets in your eye if you don't make connection.

PURPLE BOUGAINVILLEA VINE

My house in Honolulu town
Is big and cool. The roof is brown.
It once was red but now the sun
Has faded it. The vines have run
In purple splendour everywhere.
They look so fine, I do not care
To tear their gorgeous blossoms down
And paint the roof. I like it brown.

POINCIANA REGIA TREE

Regal tree, you flaunt your dress of scarlet
Brazenly. You royal vermilion harlot,
Shamelessly you toss your painted petals
On the breeze. Like thin corroded metals
Are your leaves. Were you less redly splendid
Your career of wantonness were ended.

Other trees for chaster colors labor.
They all think you're not a proper neighbor.

FOOTSTEPS

A winding Honolulu street
Goes by my house. I hear the feet
Of seven nations passing by.
I hear their footsteps fall and try
To see the people. I am blind
And have to see them in my mind.

    I hear the soft and silken swish
    Of Chinese slippers, and I wish
    That I could see the colors gay
    The women wear. For people say
    That coats of silk and bright sateen
    With golden thread are worn. I've seen
    Them passing in my mind but, . . . oh,
    I want to really see them so.

Last night the clack of wooden shoe
Or sandal sounded and I knew
A Japanese was trotting past.
I heard the sound die out at last
And thought, because I'd heard before,
That on the *obi* that she wore
Were figures in exquisite hues . . .
Pale pink and lavenders and blues.

    I pray each day . . . I pray each night
    To God. I want . . . I want my sight!

Sometimes the hard decisive sound
Of leather heels strikes on the ground
So firm . . . so firm. I know the stride
Is that of youth. A virile pride
Vibrates in every step. His eyes
Are clean and blue, just as the skies
Are blue. I know their eager gaze
Is clear . . . not blind with murky haze.

Sometimes there comes a sound so low
I scarcely hear it . . . yet I know
That native lovers, barefoot, walk.
The whispered murmur of their talk
Drifts in. I listen and surmise
The silver moon is in their eyes.
How odd . . . if poets do not lie . . .
These lovers, too, are blind as I.

All day, all day, and through the night
I hear the people pass. I fight
To keep my soul quite free from hate.
I can not yet. I cry the fate
That took my sight. Oh, if I pray
To God, and live my prayers, some day
Will He . . . if I believe . . . will He
Give back my eyes . . . my sight . . . to me?

GLAMOUR'S GONE

To a Tourist Who Could Find No Lure or Charm in Hawaii.

What thin and tepid blood must flow in veins of you
who say the glamour's gone
From all these fair far islands of the seas beneath the
Southern Cross.
 If there is not a scarlet witchery in the perfume of
 ylang-ylang . . .
 if all the lingering sweetness of white ginger blooms
 has lost its subtle thrill . . .
 if scented moonlight, vibrant with the throbbing song
 of hot native voices can not raise the rhythm of your
 heart one beat . . .
 if thrushes, singing poignant beauty in lost blue valleys of Manoa can not make you dream of Pan . . .
 if all the secret whisperings of palms, and sighing
 swooning croon of restless surf on beaches made for
 all the lovers in the world, are naught to you . . .
 if with white coral and fine gold sand you can not
 build the castle of your dreams . . .

if your cold flesh can still be calm beneath the silk
caresses of scent-burdened breezes . . .
if your light fancy can not climb the sky-flung curve
of that pale moonstone arch, the lunar rainbow, to
steal one jewelled star for your sweet love . . .
if one long sobbing note of steel guitar, slid from a
moaning minor to a tremulous treble sigh, can not
search out your slow-beating pulse and trip its slug-
gish pulsing for one quick moment . . .
if all these things have lost their power . . . for they
are not gone . . . then romance is dead, beauty is a
hag, love is an idle tale, blood can know no sultry
fevers of desire . . .

   and glamour's gone from Hawaii
   and from all the world . . .
   for you!

KOA TREES IN A MIST

Moon-mists, like veils of sheer and tinted gauze,
    Sweep down the slopes of Tantalus at night,
    Shimmer and catch the opalescent light,
Drifting like souls of ghosts, without a pause;

Floating like filmy garments of a breeze,
    Frightened and moon-mad. Endlessly they pale
    And dim and pass. Their phantom draperies trail
Tatters of silver in the koa trees.

RISING MOON

The moon is a great gold coin tossed to those ragged
vagabonds, the clouds.

SUNSET OVER WAIANAE MOUNTAINS

The white clouds lift their pale faces and blush rosily
to see the sun disrobe.

BABY STREET

A real street down Palama way in the tenement district of
Honolulu.

I walk quite slowly down Baby Street,
Babies are everywhere . . . under my feet,
Sprawled on the sidewalks, perched on the walls,
Babies in dydies, in blue overalls,
Babies in rompers of flowered cretonne,
Babies with not much of anything on,
Little brown babies in brown mamas' laps,
Philippine babies, Koreans and Japs,
Fresh shiny babies right out of the tub,
Babies in scandalous need of a scrub,
Baby Hawaiians, the sons of a chief,
Rastus from Africa, black past belief,
Babies with yellow hair, babies with brown,
Babies with just a few patches of down,
Toddling babies on little bowed legs,
Very new babies, much balder than eggs,
Portuguese babies and Russians as well,
Babies whose ancestors no one can tell,
Toothless as turkeys, these tiny young tads,
But grinning as though they were dentifrice ads.

Walk very carefully . . . make your step hesitant.
One of these babies someday may be president.

SEA BUTTERFLIES

Gay little fishes with painted scales,
Gossamer fins and chiffon tails,
Spattered with jewel dust, stained with dyes,
Gems of jade and jet for eyes.

Striped with orange and smeared with blue,
Dipped in the rainbow's every hue.
Little ones, yellow as buttercups,
Big ones, ugly as gutter-pups,
Fat ones, bloated and marked like toads,
Squatted by submarine forest roads.

Fishes gilded with guinea-gold,
Shaped like mythical beasts of old,
Some are enamelled like cloisonne,
Lacquered and penciled with colors gay.
'Broidered and traced like a Persian shawl,
Fishes that swim and fishes that crawl,
Splotched and daubed in a cubist scheme,
Some are born of a mad man's dream.
Fishes with whiskers and fishes with horns
Just like the fabulous unicorn's.
Colors that burn like a funeral pyre,
Colors as pale as a moonstone's fire,
Ochre and amethyst, ultramarine,
Amber, umber and macaw green,
Fragments of fancy, living a day,
Going their curious deep-sea way.

Gay little fishes with painted scales,
Long may you wave your chiffon tails.

HONOLULU CURRY

Lobster curry on mounds of rice . . .
If you like curry it's mighty nice
With grated cocoanut, feathered down,
Little green onions frizzled brown,
Nuts, and the yolks of hard-boiled eggs,
Mango chutney and garlic pegs,
Anchovy paste and Bombay duck,
Bits of bacon and Hindu truck,
Minced green peppers and chow-chow, too,
And anything else that occurs to you.

Mix together . . . a heaping plate.
A dish for a blinking potentate.

DIAMOND HEAD

The empty setting for some great jewel of the sun
torn from its resting place centuries before time began.

KILAUEA, the volcano.

Patterns of fury, etched in flame.

SOMEWHERE ON PUNCHBOWL HILL

A little reckless narrow street
Goes plunging down the hill to meet
The broad and stately avenue
(a thing no proper street should do.)
But does this little street repine
And moan about its swift decline
Oh, no indeed. Instead, it flaunts
A gaudy flowered dress, and taunts
The avenue below with hints
Of bougainvillea's strident tints
And poinciana's regal flame.
Why, with a brazen lack of shame
It wears a jade-green bracelet
Of "chain-of-love," the bold coquette!
The houses all along the way
Don't quite approve of such display
For they are filled (and here's the joke)
With very nice and proper folk.

CLEARING OF A KONA STORM

Storm-clouds, like muffled purple thunder, pass
Blown by the kona. Mountainous they mass
Against the sky in the sultry wrath.
Leaving across the frightened sea a path
Of silence. While, with baffled fury spent
In angry billowings, they rear their heads and vent
Their rage in futile mutterings above the land;
Then silently and sullenly disband.

PALM TREES

Long lines of patient yearning palms keep faithful
rendezvous with faithless lover-winds beside the sea.

LUΛU, AN HAWAIIAN FEAST

Oh we're going to a luau
To a luau, to a luau
    Where we'll dance the hula-hula
    On a beach beneath the stars,
And there'll be a lot of singing
For the singing boys are bringing
    All their tricky ukuleles
    And their sobbing steel guitars.

HULA MOONS

HULA DANCERS

I watched a hula-dance last night
Upon a beach of sand so white
Its crescent reproduced the moon.
The surf with driving crash and swoon
Set up a rhythm in my blood.
Kukui torches cast a flood
Of murky orange light that played
About the dancers as they swayed.

A-thud-a-thud . . . a beaten gourd!
Warm voices . . . native voices . . . poured
Wild cadences of old refrains
Like ti-root liquor in my veins.

I watched the dance . . .

                . . . a thousand years
Turned back and dully in my ears
I heard the low hypnotic beat
Of hollow drum and smelled the sweet

Sick reek of living sacrifice
And flowers crushed and burning spice;
I knew the savage prayer and chant
Of priests. I heard the victim pant
In agony. One glimpse I had
Of postures passionate and mad.

The movements of the dance last night
Were gestures from some phallic rite
Performed a thousand years ago
Before some stone-faced god, I know.

ALA MOANA

The sea is a cloth of silver
Stirred to uneasy ripples
By the ghost-white hand of the moon.
Dim in the jewelled distance
Diamond Head crouches,
A headless sphinx
Baring her tawny breasts
To the massed clouds and the sky. . . .
Mists pass
Leaving us alone with the moon
And one brief moment of ecstasy.

MY HAWAIIAN GARDEN

I plant my flowers, row on row,
In hope that they will grow just so,
All neat and sweet, but I forget
That while the phlox and mignonette
Are used to garden ways and know
The proper way that they should grow,
These tropic blossoms will not do
The sort of thing I want them to.

The yellow alamanda sprawls
In gold confusion on the walls
And in among its flower-suns
The little starry jasmine runs.
The bougainvillea climbs the trees
And flings its tatters on the breeze
All scarlet and magenta-red . . .
A canopy above my head.

The multi-colored little phlox
Grow here and there among the rocks
Like gay confetti tossed about
In some moonlit midsummer's rout.
The fragile spider-lily weaves
A cobweb lace of white. The leaves

Of croton hedges growing here
Hold autumn colors through the year.
In spring the mangoes' varnished green
Is changed to bronze. I've often seen
A honey-moth with searching tongue
And whirring wings fly in among
The heavy nodding ragged heads
Of dahlias. I have several beds
Of asters, purple, pink and white.
My ginger plants are my delight.
No flower grows so sweet and clean
As wild white ginger blooms. They mean
Hawaii to me. I make a *lei*
Of them for friends who go away.

The gay and festive "chain-of-love"
Flaunt leafy chains of hearts above
My garden gate. Day lilies show
Their throats of orange-gold. I know
Where pirates' loot, the "cup-of-gold"
Grows in my garden. They unfold
The heavy petals drenched with dew
And perfume. Morning-glories blue
Swing pale day-moons in graceful lines
About the place. Moon-flower vines
Make mimic moons with scented discs
Of petal-silk. A lizard frisks

All in and out among the blooms
A gray and graceful palm-tree looms
Above the flower beds. Its fronds
Are mirrored in my lily ponds
Where water-hyacinths have grown.
   A spiny cactus stands alone
In grim unfriendly prickliness.
I did not like it, I confess,
Until a little timid vine
Of jasmine started to entwine
The gaunt unlovely plant. They look
Like figures in my fairy-book.
(the ugly Beast is quite content
with Beauty's gentle prisonment.)

   Hibiscus hedges line my walk
With flowers. Some are white as chalk,
Or red as rouge, or pink as dawn,
Or yellow, flame, cerise or fawn.
A thousand shapes, a thousand shades.
The bees make sudden buzzing raids
Upon the orange sweetheart vine.
Against the wall I have a line
Of tall poinsettia plants. They blow
At Christmas time . . . a swaying row
Of gay fantastic jagged flowers.
On sunny days I sit for hours.

And watch the golden shower trees
Yield all their treasure to the bees.
The yellow petals strew the ground
And wax begonias grow around
A little rockery where ferns
And air-plants hang from Chinese urns.

There are no days throughout the year
Without some sort of flowers here
In sweet profusion, uncontrolled.
If all their many names were told
You'd weary of the endless list.
No color, tint or shape is missed
In Nature's wondrous gift to me.

I wonder if I've made you see
This sun-lit, moon-witched, rainbow place
Of beauty. Just a little space
Quite filled with flowers, vines and trees,
Walled in with stone, the haunt of bees
And butterflies and lunar moths.
When you are passing will you pause
Or—if you will—drop in and see
This garden that belongs to me.

NIGHT-BLOOMING CEREUS

Written for Lillian Wilder

Note. As the scarred and calloused fingers of a Chinese jade carver hold delicately the exquisite product of his art, so do the ugly cacti offer tentatively and in the night the rare unearthly beauty of their bloom.

Six months the long green cactus branches sprawl
  Like spiny serpents carved from opaque jade,
Gorging themselves with sunlight on the wall
  Or seeking dewy coolness in the shade.

Half of a year's white moons yield pallid light;
  Dews of a hundred mornings keep them fresh;
Mists cool their sun-parched skin throughout the night;
  Earth with volcanic ashes feeds their flesh.

Then on some mystic night . . . who gives the
    hour . . .
    Down the long line a silent call is thrilled;
Ten thousand buds to moonlit glory flower;
    Then thousand star-white blooms with light are filled.

Down from the mountain peaks in phantom line
    Great bronzy Polynesian gods pass by
To drink from flower-chalices a wine
    Of white and scented moonlight of Hawaii.

Dawn with its rosy eager thirsting lips
    Hurries the sun but finds the wine-cups drained;
Finds but the dregs and, disappointed, sips
    And waits 'til six new moons have waxed and waned.

HOW TO KNOW HAWAII

Oh, you'll never know Hawaii 'til you've kissed an
     Island girl
And she's hung a ginger *lei* about your neck;
'Til you've danced the hula-hula on a beach of sand and
     pearl
And have eaten *opihis* by the peck.

'Til you've hung your every garment on a big *kamani*
     tree
And have felt the foaming surf about your knees;
'Til you've plunged into the breakers with a cry of
     pagan glee
In a bathing suit of moonlight and a breeze.

'Til you've seen the lunar rainbow's phantom arch
     across the blue
And have watched the Southern Cross dip in the sea;
'Til the singing boys have stabbed your heart with
     music . . . thru and thru;
  'Til you've raced the silver surf at Waikiki;

'Til you've slid down Ginger Jack . . . and every
     youngster knows the place;
  'Til you've gorged on pig until you couldn't think;
'Til you've seen the path of fury strewn with white-hot
     lava lace
And where red Pele walks at Kilauea's brink.

'Til you've heard the old folks yarning of the days be-
    fore today;
  At a *luau* over bowls of fish and *poi;*
'Til you've gone aboard a steamer with intent to stay
    away
  And have learned the meaning of "Aloha oe."

'Til you've been so blinking homesick for these Islands
    of the Sea
  That you simply couldn't stand it any more
And you've chucked your things together . . . bought a
    ticket on the run
  And have headed for Hawaii's sunny shore.

'Til you've felt your tonsils quiver when the tears begin
    to start
  As old Diamond Head looms black against the sky;
No, you're just a *malihini* 'til you've felt down in your
    heart
  That your home . . . I mean your *home* is in Hawaii.

LEIS . . . FOR REMEMBRANCE

Written for Leatrice Joy

Will you remember when you go away
The fragrance of ginger blooms in a white lei?
Will you remember the blue of the sea
That melts into sapphires at Waikiki?
Will you remember how you used to wear
Pikoki like ivory wound in your hair?
Will you remember the moon in the trees;
The scent of gardenias borne on the breeze;
Sunsets from Tantalus, rainbows at sea;
Will you . . . I hope you will not . . . forget me?
Will you remember the shadowy beams
Of Vagabond's House in our city of dreams?
Will you remember the tropical nights
With native boys singing? The flickering lights
Of fisherman prowling about on the reef?
Will you remember . . . the moment is brief . . .
When your ship sails away while your friends on the
    shore
Sing "Aloha, farewell, 'til we see you once more."

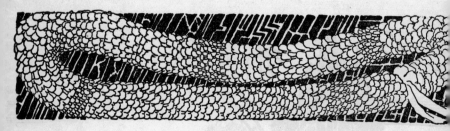

VAGABOND'S LOOT

VAGABOND'S LOOT

Worthless treasures and priceless trash,
Silver that gleams in the lightning's flash.
Gold that the sunset spills on the sky,
Gauzes and tissues in mists trailing by,
Diamonds, a necklace of dew on the grass,
Filagree silver in frost on the glass,
Lace in *kiawe* trees shadowing brooks,
Riches a money-blind man overlooks,
Perfumes of araby scenting a lane,
Opals that fall from the sky in the rain,
Gold in the sands of a shallow lagoon
Platinum dripping cold white from the moon,
Silk in the rose petals flung on the breeze,
Velvet in moss on the trunks of the trees,
Day-dreams and memories, moments acute
With thrice-distilled happiness. . . . vagabond's loot.

TO DON MAY

A friend who climbed mountains with me

We knew the desolation of great heights
And the contentment of deep valleys;
We saw the moon leap silver from the mountain peaks
And watched the red sun die in a welter of mists on the
    horizon;
We knew the white swift decline of vast snow-fields
And the small beauty of forest flowers;
Our dreams rose with the smoke of our camp fires in the
    wilderness
And our friendship glowed with the embers of fir-fires;
We shared hunger, thirst and the great struggle to-
    ward the mountain top
As we shared peace, good food and pleasant rest of our
    night camps;
All these things . . . the dizziness of sudden precipices,
    straining muscles, weariness, exaltation, the
    soothing fragrance of pine trees, the chatter of
    mountain streams and the roar of furious rapids
    entered into the pattern of our friendship and made
    it fine.
These things we knew together. . . .
And these things we will remember.

TWILIGHT

Now that the shadows of twilight are stealing into the corners of my room I'll open the covers of my favorite books, then, if I sit very still and watch through the weaving gray magic of my cigarette smoke I may see those well-loved characters stepping quietly forth from the thumbed pages. . . .

Kim, sunbrowned and impish, vagabonding in the bazaars of India and finding fine life on the high-road to Simla.

Huckleberry Finn, heart-brother of Kim, floating on a raft in the Mississippi, poet and great dreamer. . . .

Salammbo, wandering in drugged mystic ecstasy among the white peacocks on the terraces above Carthage. . . .

Salome with rouged fingertips pressed against her gilded eye-lids brooding on her erotic passion for Jokannan. . . .

Sonnica of Saguntum tossing the bright bauble of life into the fires of a great renunciation. . . .

Pale Pelleas and paler Melisande suffering the strange fevers of their love. . . .

Galahad, Eve and earthy Adam . . .

Eben Holden, d'Artagnan and Carmen . . .

Moby Dick and Kamehameha. . . .

Camille and Guinivere. . . .

Jurgen and Helen of Troy. . . .

Cigarette and Joan the Maid. . . .

Judith of Bethulia. . . .

Perseus with borrowed wings for his heels. . . .

The raw Yankee who made folly of King Arthur's
court. . . .
Fagin the Jew and Pere Goriot. . . .
Dorian Gray with his strange perverse life. . . .
Dracula. . . .
John Silence, doctor of souls. . . .
Sheba. . . .

One by one they whisper their curious stories until I
turn on the lights of evening, arch-enemy of dreams.
Even then they are not really gone. If I listen I can hear
the rustle of their garments, the echoes of their laughter
and the faint murmur of their voices in the corner by
the book-shelves.

FROM A JAVANESE BATIK

Somewhere white peacocks dream on pedestals of
   twisted brass
Or spread their pale fantastic fans beneath the perfumed ylang-ylang;
Somewhere slim maidens in their gilded garments pass
   Strumming the yalvi . . . chanting to its slow barbaric twang.

HAWAIIAN DRIFTWOOD

Some of us drift to these shores on the trade-winds;
   Drift here and linger. The days slip along,
Autumn and summer, the spring and the winter
   Pass like the uncounted notes of a song.

Some of our hearts find their roots here and blossom.
   Harder each day to depart if one lingers,
Hours and days and the months and the seasons
   Trickle like water and sand through our fingers.

SOMEDAY

A request to Earl Challenger

Someday when Death with sudden callous hands
  Strikes from my grasp the vibrant gift of life,
Shatters the crystal, stills my hot demands
  For songs of color and the surge of strife,
    Chills the warm blood and numbs this flesh of mine,
      Stifles the laugh that answers death with mirth;
    Withers the lips that drink love's rouge-red wine,
      Blurs the quick senses, renders all to earth,
Then you who are my friend take what remains
  When searing flames have had their cruel way
And go to that high place where summer rains
  And moonmists drift and lunar-rainbows play,
    There with a few gay ghosts of memories,
      Shadows of joys we knew, bid quick farewell
    And scatter my futile ashes on the breeze
      To float to Heaven or to drift to Hell
For this will be a restless dust of mine
  Seeking the places that I loved and knew,
Haunting the beaches golden wavered line,
  Searching the glades where ginger blossoms grew,
    Wandering down the trade-wind's vagrant way,
      Riding the surf's onrushing jade-green crest,
    'Til on a future blessed lazy day
      My tired spirit finds gray dreamless rest.

ICARUS

To a good friend and gallant flier who crashed

They failed, those man-made wings! Then down the
    graying sky
A living meteor fell with cruel speed. A cry
Part fear but greater part farewell to all dear things
Joined with the screaming of wind-tortured wings;
Farewell to clouds and clean high places of the blue;
Farewell to sunlight, gallant daring flight. He knew
The hurt of treachery when trusted pinions turned
To futile webs of tattered gauze. He learned
In those swift seconds all that man may hope to know
Of grandeur and of sorrow. This I feel is so
That ere death's anæsthesia blurred away
All consciousness of hope, regret, dismay,
He looked into his heart and visioned there
Only a thankfulness for answered prayer
That as crusader of the blue unconquered sky,
Having so bravely lived, so might he bravely die.

TWO WHO FOLLOWED THE PATH OF THE SUN

Maitland and Hegenberger, the first to fly from America to Hawaii.

The red sun saw them rise, fearless and strong
Into the still blue sky, and all day long
The ceaseless drone of motors stirred the air,
A great defiant challenge. Clear and fair
With pageantry of banners then, the sun
Sank to the sea, reluctant to be done
With that brave sight. It paved a path with gold
To guide the flyers down the west. The cold
White stars took up the vigil through the night
And watched with dazzled eyes the steady flight.
Then they unwillingly gave way. The second dawn
Flared with new splendour on the pathway drawn
Across the pathless sea. Gladly the sun
Welcomed the dauntless men . . . their victory won.

MOTHER

Dear frail gray Mother with your quiet hands
  Reposed in patient waiting as the days slip by;
  A tired Dresden figure stifling a sigh
To smile a gallant answer to the years' demands.

I've watched relentless time make gold depart
  From your bright hair and fade your roses' hue;
  It could not dim your brave eyes' dauntless blue
Nor break the high fine courage of your heart.

You are my one strong faith . . . you can not fail;
  The vagabond's one love that can not die.
  You'd leave blue Heaven if you heard my cry
To turn a guiding star-gleam on the trail.

FOREBODING

For Drum Accompaniment

... zoom ... zoom ... zoom ...
   that is the sound of the surf ...
as the great green waves rush up the shore
with a murderous thundering ominous roar
and leave drowned dead things at my door
   ... zoom ... zoom ... zoom ...

   ... suish ... suish ... shuis-s-h ...
   that is the sound of the tow ...
as it slips and slithers along the sands
with terrible groping formless hands
that drag at my beach-house where it stands
   ... suish ... suis-s-h ... suis-s-sh ...

   eeeie-u-u ... eeeie-u-u- ... eeeie-u-u- ...
   that is the sound of the wind
it wails like a banshee adrift in space
and threatens to scatter my driftwood place.
it slashes the sand like spite in my face
   eeeie-u-u-u ... eeeie-u-u ... eeeie-u-u ...

   Surf ... tow ... or the wind ...
   which of the three will it be ...
the surf ... will it bludgeon and beat me dead ...
or the tow drag me down to its ocean bed ...
or the wind wail a dirge above my head ...
   zoom ... suis-s-h ... eeeie-u-u. ...

HOLLYWOOD

Hollywood . . . Hollywood . . .
Fabulous Follywood . . .
Celluloid Babylon, glorious, glamorous,
    City delirious,
    Frivolous, serious,
Goal of ambitious and vicious and clamorous.

    Here are the infamous,
    Innocent, sinfamous,
Striving, conniving to gain recognition,
    Faddists, fanatics
    And men who make batiks,
Trying and crying in mad competition.

    Millionaire movie queens,
    Milliners, Magdalenes,
Movie-bug bitten, a fatal affliction.
    Eager young extra girls,
    Sinuous sextra girls,
Fighting for fame in the flickering fiction.

    Beauties from Budapest,
    Bangor and Bucharest,
Cuties from Cairo in lovely profusion.
    Scripts and scenarios,
    Leering Lotharios,
Grease-paint and gossamer, dreams and illusion.

Treachery, loyalty,
Celluloid royalty,
Pickfords and Chaplins, de Milles and the Gishes,
Stars meteoric,
Romantic, caloric,
Peers in the kingdom of visions and wishes.

Drama, a city full,
Tragic and pitiful,
Bunk, junk and genius amazingly blended.
Tawdry, tremendous,
Absurd and stupendous,
Shoddy and cheap . . . and astoundingly splendid.

Hollywood . . . Hollywood,
Fabulous Follywood . . .
Target for censor, reformer and deacon.
They say you're a harlot,
Your sins are as scarlet
Perhaps you're a goddess that bears a bright beacon.

FIRE IN ICE

To F. H. L. . . . a most unusual lady, as coldly intellectual
as she is warmly beautiful.

You are a silver thread across a web of mauve and rose.

A fleck of foam riding triumphant on the malestrom of
    emotion.

The thin tense cry of a violin to the contralto of a cello.

The cold gleam of a diamond in the fever of opals.

A fine blue vein across a hot red artery.

Shimmer of moonstones in a goblet of wine.

An arrow of ice aslant a summer pool.

Amber beads on a chain of platinum.

Cut crystal between rubies.

Frost on pomegranates.

Fire in ice.

Suppose the ice of you
Melted in the fire of you.
What would you be
Damp ashes!
You would not interest me
Probably.

PHILANDERER

Love me, Love, but love me lightly.
  Weave no silken gauze to tie me.
I acknowledge most contritely
  Vows are bonds that irk and try me.

If you find a strand enfolds me,
  Flick a careless finger through it.
Break the gossamer that holds me
  But, be sure I see you do it.

Then, because I think you flout me,
  I will take the bond you sever
And I'll bind it close about me
  For a while . . . if not forever.

PRODIGAL'S SONG

I'm glad I drank the blood-red wine,
    The crimson froth, the murky dregs,
I'm glad I drank the amber ale
    That bubbled forth from wooden kegs.

I'm glad I squandered folly's gold
    On worthless treasure, priceless trash,
I'm glad I danced the nights away
    To frenzied cymbals' blatant crash.

I'm glad I kissed soft painted lips,
    I'm glad I knew responsive flesh,
I'm glad I burned the vital flame
    While fire of life was in me fresh.

I'm glad I know the look of Heav'n,
    I'm glad I had a slant at Hell,
I'm glad I lived, I'm glad I loved
    Before the slow black curtain fell.

I'm glad that I can madly laugh,
    I'm glad that I don't give a damn
To see myself . . . a tawdry thing.
    I'm glad. Oh God! Like Hell I am.

AFTERMATH

I sat throughout the long ungodly night
   Watching the moon climb blindly in the sky;
   Watching gaunt gray Regret cry wildly by;
Watching Remorse with futile Longing fight.

Tortured and mad, my thoughts made ghastly play,
   Weaving a tangled web with twisted skeins
   Of sorrow. Through my chilled and tortured veins
Flowed a slow poison, shame thinned with dismay.

Dawn, with its golden flood of cleansing light
   Brought small relief. The gray grim wraiths withdrew
   To secret hiding, only to renew
Their morbid dance with coming of the night.

AT A LUAU, HAWAIIAN FEAST

Can't you feel the happy tingle. . . .
Can't you hear the snappy jingle
  Of the jazzy ukulele . . . it's a cheerful sound and
    pert.
Can't you hear the deeper throbbing
And the sentimental sobbing
  Of the steel guitars a-crying like a laugh that hides
    a hurt.

On the tables, *leis* of *mai-le*
Sweetly fragrant peeping shyly
  From the blazing red hibiscus and the mountain-
    green of *ti*
How your appetite does quicken
When you see the bowls of chicken.
  And the *poi* . . . oh boy . . . why some folks never
    like it puzzles me.

See the salty mounds of *limu*
And the pig hot from the *imu;*
  See the smoking sweet potatoes and the mullet
    wrapped in leaves.
Little nips of roast *kukui,*
Squid and *luau,* rich and gooey.
  That's the thing you praise to folks away and nobody
    believes.

Fresh *opihis* there to munch on;
Little crabs to crack and crunch on;
  Shrimp and lobster, luscious *wana*. What comes last
    and what comes first.

Use your fingers . . . don't be fussy
Though it is a trifle mussy;
  You'll enjoy it and you'll gorge yourself until you
    nearly burst.

Here's a cup . . . don't ask what's in it.
Drink it down and in a minute
  You'll be gayer than the gayest with your troubles
    left behind.
See those smiling kindly faces.
Well, I've been a lot of places
  But I've never found a welcome like the Honolulu
    kind.

There's the moon just faintly showing
Through the torches' orange glowing.
  Some one sing a song . . . an old song . . . not this
    modern whah-whah jazz.
"Imi au" that song of longing
Sets old memories to thronging.
  There's a poignancy about it that no other love song
    has.

Getting late . . . a few are yawning.
In the sky a hint of dawning.
  Gone the fish and pig and *luau,* gone the bowls of
    creamy poi.
Don't you hate to hear them starting
That one perfect song of parting
  Like a plucking on your heart-strings " 'Til we meet,
    Aloha oe."

TO LEILEHUA

Who caught the poetry of Hawaii in her hula-dance.

Swift-changing curves. The gestures of her hands
Taught waves to draw white lines upon the sands.

Slim fingers, tipped like gulls' wings bent in flight;
Dark tropic eyes, deep sky-black pools of night.

Slow fluid curves. A body young and gay . . .
A flower watched her dance and learn to sway.

From throat to wrist . . . sweet slipping wilting lines
That stole their grace from wind-waved mai-le vines.

Her dance, a mystic half-forgotten rite
Before some Polynesian god at night.

HOMESICK FOR THE FAIR ISLANDS

In New York

Today I passed a tiny florist shop
With hurried step . . . a fragrance made me stop
And look with sudden wistful homesick stare.
A bowl of pale gardenias beckoned there
Behind the glass. So white! So deeply green
The leaves. Auwe, how often have I seen
The hedges starred with those soft velvet flowers.
How often has their fragrance perfumed hours
Of high romance in Flappers Acre, Waikiki,
Auwe! I'm homesick as can be.

DAWN IN THE ISLANDS

Black out of blackness. Mountains taking form.
  The sun behind gray clouds. A hint of rain.
  And colors seeping into things again.
Shy green, pale blue and yellow, thinly warm.

SECRET PLACE

There's a place in Manoa, way up in the hills,
  Where the forest comes down like an army in green;
Where the gossamer sheen of a waterfall spills
    And is flung by the breeze
    To the rocks and the trees
And the thrushes, shy singers, are heard and not seen.

It is there that the ginger blows, fragrant and white;
  Where climbing *lianas* trail down from the sky;
And the ferns make a canopy, lacy and light;
    There's a spring that is cool
    Flowing into a pool
And a gay little brook that goes burbling by.

The shadows that fall from the leaves to the grass
  Are rags of black velvet on emerald plush
And the clouds dim the sunlight to gray as they pass
    Where the day filters through
    To the slender bamboo
And a sly, slinky mongoose slips out of the brush.

If I look through the curtains of leaves hanging down
　I can see tiny glimmers of dazzling blue
And patches of turquoise and blotches of brown
　　With spatters of yellow
　　And orange and mellow;
　The sea and the sky and the roofs of the town.

It is quiet and peaceful and restful and cool;
　It's secret, it's mine, this lost little spot;
I go there to think and to dream by the pool
　　All alone, quite, unless . . .
　　I don't blush to confess
That it's nicer with someone I love a whole lot.

BROCADE

What is the pattern and fabric of our love?
Moonlight, drawn through silver mists,
By the witchery of night-winds on Tantalus.
  Darkly velvet the shadows of koa leaves
Fall in curved delicacy, shifting and touching
Like lips that lightly touch and touch again.
Raindrops pierce the dimly shadowed lines
Like crystal beads tossed across an old and lovely
      tapestry.
  In swift-flowing line, clean, glinting,
Runs the red-gold thread of ecstasy
And by it the twilight mauve of sadness
Giving the rich gold a brighter gleam.
Here and there, in no arranged design,
Are rare fine jewels. . . .
Fire-opals, burning with a lambent flame,
Amethysts deeply purple as a sorrow,
Lapis, bluely restful,
And one deep sapphire
Holding in its heart a white radiance
Like that first star we saw at evening . . .
  These are our little moments of happiness.

FRAGMENT

Some day in some cold city of the north
I'll hear the tattered fragment of a song,
"Aloha oe." The dull gray city streets will **fade.**
I'll see the lavish gold of summer's suns
Drenching a land of joyous fadeless green;
I'll see the luminous Hawaiian moons
Making white magic with the sea and sky;
I'll sense the fragrance of white ginger;
I'll see that single burning star
That leaves a silver path across the sea
At Waikiki.
In some cold city of the north I'll hear that song
And one, not more than one pale moon will wane
Then I'll be back.

WHAT IS HAWAII?

Shadows of trade-clouds racing on the sand,
   Nights that are webs of moonlight spun with song,
Bridges of rainbows joining sky and land,
   Days that are hours . . . hours eons long.
Thundering surf in grand exalted chant,
   Suns that are guinea gold and moons of brass,
Copperous dawns and sunsets palpitant
   Pulsing with color. Kona storms that pass,
Frantic and frenzied, tarnishing the sea,
   Bellowing challenge to the surf's mad roar,
Dying in distant purple pageantry
   Leaving the land more smiling than before.
Sunlight and shadow, stars and veiling mist,
   Moody, uncertain, mingled tears and smiles.
When I'm away my heart keeps faithful tryst
   With my far, pagan, thrice-enchanted isles.

TO ONE HOUR OF ONE NIGHT

To one hour of one night
between the setting of a tired moon
and the rising of a joyous sun
I dedicate this poem.

Ah, you were lovely . . . lovely on that last mad night
With all your flesh white-gold and golden-white
Wearing a robe of moon-mist traced with shadow-leaves,
Caught with a spray of jasmine-stars whose perfume
  weaves
Meshes of sweet delirium.
                    The moon was gone
Wearied as we with rapture ere the jealous dawn
Flung its barbaric banners on the tender sky.
Wisely we said farewell . . . bid swift good-bye
While still the glamour of the night was fresh
For how could I who'd known the glory of your flesh
Behold you primly garmented to meet the day.
Even caressing satin would have bruised away
The gossamer of romance that you wore for me.
Now you remain a dream-remembered ecstasy
Sweeter in each remembering. Sandra, I do
Give thanks to all the gods there are for that last hour
  of you.

Walking in beauty as we are, sun-gold, moonsilver ever
  in our eyes.
  Treading on flowers, breathing perfumed air,
We do forget what loveliness is ours, what treasure lies
  Quick to our hands until, all unaware
We come to a sudden corner, face the sea and clouds, a
  stretch of sky,
  Burning with color, drenched with glory. So,
As one, walking asleep with open eyes, wakens to a cry
  We waken to a beauty which we saw and did not
  know.

ALOHA OE

Its meaning

It's more than just an easy word for casual good-bye;
It's gayer than a greeting and it's sadder than a sigh;
It has the hurting poignancy, the pathos of a sob;
It's sweeter than a youthful heart's exquisite joyous
    throb;
It's all the tender messages that words can not convey;
It's tears unshed, and longing for a loved one gone
    away;
It's welcome to Hawaii and it's lingering farewell;
It's all the dear and silent things that lovers' lips can
    tell;
It's woven into flower *leis* and old Hawaiian songs;
It's frailer than a spider-web and strong as leather
    thongs;
It's fresh as dew on ginger blooms and older than the
    moon;
It's in the little lullabys that native mothers croon;
It's said a hundred different ways, in sadness and in
    joy;
Aloha means "I love you." So, I say "Aloha oe."

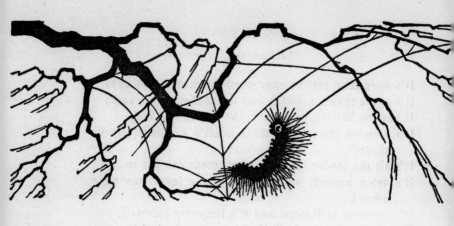

PAU

which, in Hawaiian, means finished.